Final Lap!
GO-KART RACING

Christine Dugan, M.A.Ed.

Consultants

Timothy Rasinski, Ph.D.
Kent State University

Lori Oczkus
Literacy Consultant

Dan Edmunds
Director of Automotive
Engineering

Based on writing from
TIME For Kids. *TIME For Kids* and the *TIME
For Kids* logo are registered trademarks of
TIME Inc. Used under license.

Publishing Credits

Dona Herweck Rice, *Editor-in-Chief*
Lee Aucoin, *Creative Director*
Jamey Acosta, *Senior Editor*
Heidi Fiedler, *Editor*
Lexa Hoang, *Designer*
Stephanie Reid, *Photo Editor*
Emily Engle, *Contributing Author*
Rachelle Cracchiolo, *M.S.Ed., Publisher*

Teacher Created Materials

5301 Oceanus Drive
Huntington Beach, CA 92649-1030
http://www.tcmpub.com
ISBN 978-1-4333-4832-7

Table of Contents

The Thrill
of the Ride

In 1955, Art Ingels built the first go-kart. He is sometimes called the Father of Karting. He used a lawn mower engine and scrap metal to build his first kart!

The driver looks down from the top of the hill. The road below curves sharply. The car rumbles. The flag drops, and the race starts! The driver sets off, and the **engine** roars. The fans go wild.

Go-karts are an exciting way to get around, have fun, and even race with other drivers. A go-kart is a small vehicle with four wheels. Go-karts come in many sizes and materials. They can be simple push karts without a motor, or they can be racing machines with powerful engines.

THINK LINK

Think you're ready to hit the road? Here's what you'll need to know before you get started:

- how to build a go-kart
- simple safety tips and racing rules
- the importance of math in this high-octane sport

Building a Machine

Kart or Buggy?

Go-karts are named different things around the world. They may be called *go-karts*, *buggies*, or *soapbox racers*. In Australia, they are called *billy carts*.

Many people enjoy go-karts as a hobby. They find that part of the fun is actually building the kart. Working with someone else makes it even more fun. Building go-karts requires a lot of cooperation.

Building Basics

It is important to have a plan before starting to build. This plan might be a **blueprint** of some kind. It shows what the finished kart will look like. Making a plan uses math skills. There are measurements and estimates. Calculations need to be made. Using math lets drivers build the kart that's right for them.

Within a **Fraction** of an **Inch**

People who build go-karts must make precise measurements. Parts, time, and distance must all be measured carefully.

$5\frac{?}{?}$

Parts

If part of the kart is off just a fraction of an inch, it may cause the entire kart to not function properly. Consider this example: one front wheel measures $6\frac{2}{8}$ inches across. The other front wheel measures $5\frac{7}{8}$ inches across. What is the difference in the sizes of the wheels?

6$\frac{2}{8}$

STOP! THINK...

- If a kart had front wheels of different sizes, how do you think it would affect the kart?

- Would the kart be safe to drive?

- Would the difference in size slow down the kart?

Distance

The length of the track must be measured precisely. It determines how wide the track should be, how many drivers can race at one time, and what type of race it will be.

Time

A stopwatch can time multiple racers at the same time. The timer will note each driver's time within a fraction of a second.

Nuts and Bolts

A plan for building a go-kart shows all the parts needed to make it run. The **frame** of the kart is the first part to consider. The other parts can be changed later, but the frame can't be. The frame can come in different shapes. It can be designed to help the kart move at a faster pace.

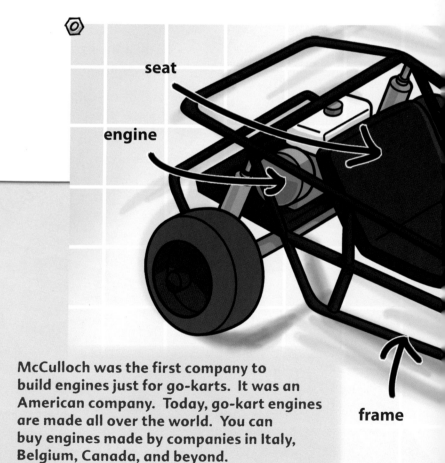

seat

engine

frame

McCulloch was the first company to build engines just for go-karts. It was an American company. Today, go-kart engines are made all over the world. You can buy engines made by companies in Italy, Belgium, Canada, and beyond.

The engine is another important part of a go-kart. It makes the kart move. The power of the engine affects how fast the kart can go. Brakes are important because they make the kart stop. A plan for a go-kart may show tires, seats, and a steering wheel, too. Following a good plan makes the building process go much more smoothly.

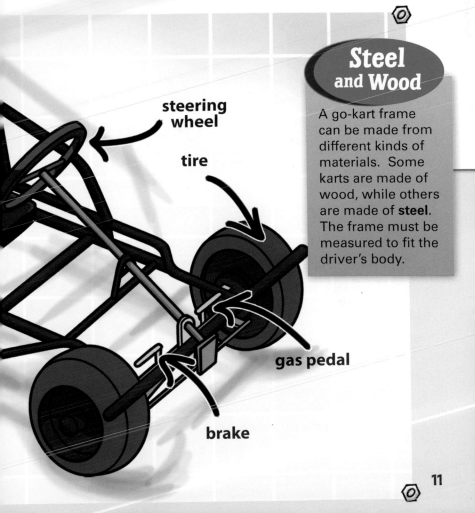

steering wheel

tire

gas pedal

brake

Steel and Wood

A go-kart frame can be made from different kinds of materials. Some karts are made of wood, while others are made of **steel**. The frame must be measured to fit the driver's body.

Awesome Angles

Fitting parts together with tools requires lots of measurements. The blueprint below shows where to measure an **angle**. An angle is the space between two **intersecting** lines. It is measured in degrees. The blueprint shows how to install the steering wheel at a 45° angle.

There is a 45° angle between the steering wheel and the floor of the kart.

45°

Additional Angles

The front wheels of the kart should be at an 85° angle for fast turns. The angles of the seat and brake will add to the driver's comfort and safety.

Go-karts come in a variety of shapes and sizes. The frame of the kart is measured so that all the parts will fit together. Look at this blueprint designed for a young driver. The perimeter is the total distance around a two-dimensional shape. What is the perimeter of this shape?

Full Power

The builder uses tools to put the parts together. Young go-kart drivers must work with an adult whenever using power tools. These tools can be very dangerous. **Safety goggles** or gloves may be needed.

Power saws and drills are often used to build a kart. A saw cuts the wood or metal for the frame. It can cut other parts of the kart, too. A drill makes holes for bolts and joins the parts together. No go-kart driver wants the kart to fall apart in the middle of a ride!

Always get an adult's help when using power tools.

Powerful Potential

Sandpaper smooths wood parts on a kart. A hammer and nails connect parts of a wood frame. These tools are not powered by electricity. They are powered by you!

Goggles protect eyes from flying scraps.

Full Throttle

The thrill of a go-kart comes from the speed of the ride. The engine and the wheels make the kart move forward. Some engines get energy from electricity. Others get it from gasoline. But not all go-karts have engines. Some are pushed down a hill. Drivers let **gravity** take over to carry them down the hill.

Give It Some Gas!

A go-kart gas tank may hold about 2 quarts of gasoline. A small car may have a tank that holds 12 gallons. There are 4 quarts in a gallon. How many quarts are in a small car tank? How many more quarts are in a small car tank than in a go-kart tank?

Burning Rubber

Most go-karts have larger tires in the back, and smaller ones up front. Smaller tires make the car easier to steer. Larger tires provide better **traction**.

The Need for Speed

A driver's heart races as the kart speeds around the course. Drivers train so they can stay calm. They need to be safe as they drive at top speeds. Different types of go-karts are built to travel safely at different speeds. Most go-karts that young drivers build can go about 20 miles per hour. Superkarts are special karts designed to go over 100 miles per hour. Superkarts are most often raced on large racetracks.

Safety Before Speed

It is important for drivers to practice in a safe area before trying to increase their speed. Drivers should know what speeds are safe for them and their karts. Going too fast can lead to unsafe conditions.

Speed and Velocity

Speed refers to how fast an object is moving. **Velocity** is the rate at which an object changes position. Velocity is measured in units of distance and time, such as miles per hour.

Velocity = Distance ÷ Time

If a kart travels at 20 miles per hour and it travels 120 miles over the course of a race, how long did the driver race in the kart?

120 miles

Screech!

If go-karts are going to move so quickly, they need to be able to slow down as well! Luckily, brakes are standard on every go-kart. Braking is a good way to stop a go-kart. Without brakes drivers would have to use their feet to stop the kart—ouch!

Most go-karts have brake pedals. Drivers use their feet to push the pedal and make the kart stop. Some go-karts have a **hand brake**. These brakes work by pulling on a **lever**. Brakes should allow a kart to stop quickly and safely. They need to work well on different surfaces. They should be tested in wet or dry conditions. Brake pads slow a vehicle by applying pressure and **friction**. Once the wheels stop turning, the vehicle also stops moving.

Pit Stop

A go-kart's brake pads last approximately 500 miles before they need to be replaced. If you have driven 238 miles on a go-kart, how many more miles do you have before you need to change the brake pads?

Have you ever seen smoke coming off a tire? This is called a *burnout*. If the tires are spinning too fast to grip the road, they create friction. The friction creates so much heat that the tires actually start to smoke!

DIG DEEPER!

Putting on the Brakes

Go-kart drivers want to drive as fast as possible. That's how they win the race! But sometimes, in order to be safe, they need to drive more slowly. The race officials use different-color flags to communicate with the drivers. This chart shows what some of the colored flags mean.

Black Flag

A driver should head to the pits immediately. It may mean he or she has be disqualified.

Blue Flag

This flag tells slower drivers to let faster karts pass.

Red and Yellow Striped Flag

Drivers are warned that the track is slippery.

The black-and-white checkered flag means the winner has crossed the finish line and the race is over.

68

Red Flag

Drivers must stop their karts and go to the pits. Conditions are too dangerous to race.

Yellow Flag

Drivers need to slow down. There is a hazard on the track.

Green Flag

Drivers can start the race. Conditions are safe.

Fast Flags

There are many other flags used in go-kart racing. A black flag with a red circle means a driver is having mechanical problems. A black-and-white flag divided on a diagonal line means a driver is not following the rules. But the flag that all drivers want to see is the checkered flag. That means they have won the race!

Smart Steering

There is much more to driving a go-kart than simply going fast and stopping. Go-kart drivers must know how to steer the kart safely. This helps them avoid crashing into other objects.

The steering wheel makes the tires move in the right direction. There are other parts within the kart that help it steer, too. Some of these parts are the **steering shaft**, **tie rods**, and wheel **spindles**. These parts work together as part of the steering system.

One important skill any driver must learn is how to turn and steer slowly and carefully. Sudden, quick turns can make a go-kart flip over.

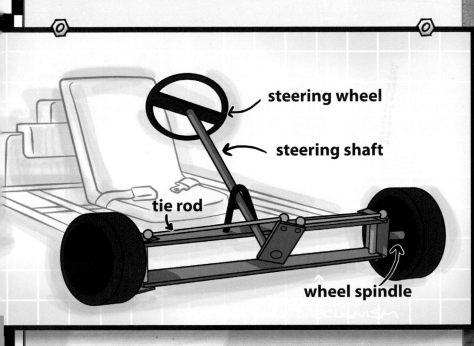

steering wheel

steering shaft

tie rod

wheel spindle

The Full 360

Go-kart drivers need to think about **turning radius** as they steer. Turning radius is the size of the smallest U-turn that a vehicle can make. The term is related to both the **radius** and the **diameter** of a circle. A go-kart moving around a track or curved path requires a small turning radius.

180°

diameter

The phrase *turning on a dime* means a car can turn in a very small space. In other words, the car has a small turning radius. The phrase refers to a dime because the dime is the smallest U.S. coin.

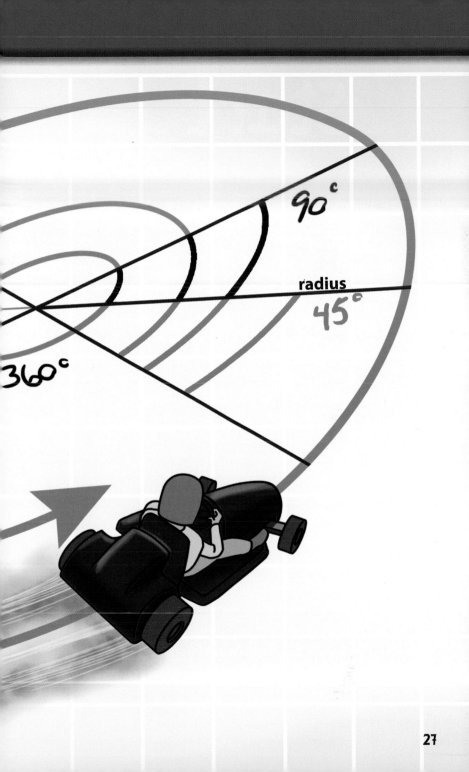

90°

radius

45°

360°

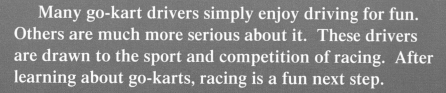

Start Your Engines

Many go-kart drivers simply enjoy driving for fun. Others are much more serious about it. These drivers are drawn to the sport and competition of racing. After learning about go-karts, racing is a fun next step.

Go-kart races take place indoors and outdoors. Drivers race on paved tracks. In between competitions, they can practice on the course. Racing requires drivers to use good judgment. They learn driving **techniques** (tek-NEEKS) so they can quickly and **efficiently** win races. Racers need to use caution when driving so close to other go-karts.

Tony Stewart

Tony Stewart is a
NASCAR driver.
NASCAR stands for
National Association
for Stock Car Auto
Racing. When he was
just eight years old, he
won his first karting
championship. In the
years that followed,
he also won the
1983 International
Karting Federation
Grand National
Championship and
the 1987 World Karting
Association National
Championship—all
before he was 18!

Crash Course

Go-karts may **collide** during a race. Karts travel near each other. Small movements can make go-karts cross paths. Drivers can also run into objects that line the course.

The faster a go-kart travels, the more serious a collision can be. It takes longer to **decelerate** (dee-SEL-uh-reyt) safely from a higher rate of speed. This is true for any type of movement. A runner or cyclist takes longer to slow down from faster speeds, too. This is why driving fast requires careful driving.

In 2000, more than 12,000 kids were injured in go-kart accidents. Smart drivers avoid accidents and protect themselves by wearing helmets.

Harnesses and Belts

Drivers should wear a safety belt whenever they drive karts. Some go-karts have a lap belt. Others have a harness belt that goes over the driver's shoulders.

Not a Toy

It is a huge responsibility to operate a moving vehicle. Bikes and scooters can travel at fast speeds, but a go-kart can go even faster. Driving a go-kart comes with serious rules and safety concerns.

Safe driving begins with using seat belts. There should never be more people in the go-kart than there are seats and seat belts. This usually means only one or two people in the kart at one time. Seat belts are never an option. They are **mandatory** for all go-kart drivers and passengers. They protect drivers from being thrown in the event of an accident.

Go-kart drivers should have fun! That is what go-karts are for, but fun comes with responsible use. It is never a good idea to get silly behind the wheel of a moving kart—someone could get hurt.

Helmet Safety

Helmets are vital for all go-kart drivers. A helmet can protect the head from rocks thrown up by other karts. It will also help keep a driver safe if a go-kart flips in a collision.

Winter Storage

Some drivers store their karts in the winter. The cold weather can make driving difficult. Drivers store their karts in a dry place. Some owners do **maintenance** work on their karts before storing them. That way, they will be ready to go when the weather warms up!

Safety Checks

Another way to be safe in a go-kart is by completing regular maintenance and safety checks. This is true for a car or even a bike, which both require regular tune-ups. All parts of the kart should be checked to make sure nothing is loose, broken, or worn. Tires must be changed when they begin to show signs of wear. Tires should have the correct amount of air and be rotated every once in a while. This keeps them from getting worn on one side. Drivers should also keep an eye on the kart frame for cracks or dents. These can be repaired to keep the frame safe. When the time comes to add fuel or check the engine, young go-kart drivers must always work with an adult.

Rotating the tire position prevents uneven wear.

After a race, a kart needs maintenance.

The Karting Community

Karting is a lot of fun. It's a great way to get involved with the racing community. There are many people who love to race go-karts, and they love to talk about racing with others. There are websites for people to share their excitement for karts.

People also travel for races. They meet other go-kart drivers. They feel connected to the racing community. And they get to see new places!

Jump Start

Go-kart racing is seen as a stepping stone to more serious forms of **motorsport**. Many professional race car drivers became interested in racing by building, driving, and racing go-karts as children.

DIG DEEPER!

Off-Road Racing

Go-kart racing is related to other kinds of motorsports. Many followers of go-kart racing also enjoy off-road vehicles. If you're ready to get dirty, check out these wild rides.

Dirt Bikes

They may look like regular motorcycles, but these bikes are built for adventure. They are lighter weight and tough enough to handle rugged **terrain**. Many dirt bikes are built without a seat.

Rally Cars

Rallying, or rally racing, is popular across Europe. Special cars, called *rally cars*, are driven by very skilled drivers. They often race on outdoor courses made of dirt, snow, ice, or gravel.

Monster Trucks

The oversize tires on these huge trucks make a big difference. They can drive over large rocks, sand dunes, and rivers.

Dune Buggies

Drivers drive these types of vehicles in beautiful places around the world. They can be raced on dirt, mud, or sand surfaces.

Baja 1000

The Baja 1000 is a popular race that happens each year. The course begins in Ensenada, Mexico. It is 1,000 miles long and goes south. Drivers race off-road vehicles such as motorcycles, dune buggies, and trucks.

Drivers Wanted

It's hard to imagine something more exhilarating than racing around a curvy course in a go-kart race. Yet building a go-kart can be just as exciting as racing one. Most go-karts out on the road were built by hand with lots of care. The construction process is just part of the fun. Fans of the sport bond with friends and family as they work together. They make a plan to create a safe kart that moves fast and handles well. Today's go-karts can handle all the twists and turns in the track. Building and racing go-karts is a fun way to get out on the track and zoom ahead. Anyone looking for an adventure should put the pedal to the metal and hit the track.

License to Drive

Are you too young to drive a car? Well, maybe you can drive a go-kart! A go-kart allows young people to drive a vehicle before the law does. A go-kart should be built to fit the age and experience of the person who will be driving it.

Let's Go!

Maybe you can't build your own kart, but you can still satisfy your need for speed. There are many indoor tracks. You can learn to drive a go-kart in a safe environment. Plus, you can have a lot of fun with your friends and family!

Glossary

angle—the space between two intersecting lines

blueprint—a plan or guide for how to build something

collide—to hit a person or object

decelerate—to slow down

diameter—a straight line from one side of a circle through the center to the other side

efficiently—doing something well with minimal energy

engine—a machine that powers equipment

frame—a group of parts arranged to give form or support to something

friction—the rubbing of one object or surface against another

gravity—the force of attraction between two objects that have mass

hand brake—a lever that can be pulled to stop a vehicle

intersecting—meeting or cutting across or through

lever—a long handle that you push or pull to make a machine stop or start

maintenance—continued repair work, upkeep

mandatory—essential; required

motorsport—a sport in which participants race motor vehicles, usually around a track

radius—a straight line from the center of a circle to any point at its edge

safety goggles—plastic glasses worn to protect the eyes

spindles—the part of the steering system connected to the wheels

steel—a hard, strong, durable form of iron

steering shaft—the part of the steering system connected to the steering wheel

techniques—methods or ways of doing something

terrain—a piece of land; ground

tie rods—metal arms that connect the steering shaft to the spindles

traction—the friction between a moving object and the surface on which it is moving

turning radius—the size of the smallest U-turn that a vehicle can make

velocity—the rate at which an object changes position

Index

Bibliography

Blomquist, Christopher. *Motocross in the X Games.*
PowerKids Press, 2003.

This book tells about the off-roading motorcycle sport called Motocross
and how riders compete in this sport during the X Games.

Bridgewater, Gill and Julian Bridgewater. *The Soapbox
Bible: How to Build Your Own Soapbox, Buggy, or
Go-Cart.* **Sterling Publishing Co., Inc., 2010.**

This book contains plans and blueprints for creating a variety of different
karts, such as soapboxes, buggies, or go-karts. Difficulty ranges from
assembling with ready-made components to building the entire vehicle
from scratch.

David, Jack. *Go-kart Racing.* **Children's Press, 2008.**

Learn about the exciting sport of karting, including the history of the
sport, technology, and the different types of competitions that go-karts are
raced in.

Gidley, Memo and Jeff Grist. *Karting: Everything You
Need to Know.* **Motorbooks, 2006.**

With tips on maintenance, safety equipment, and the basics of getting
started, this book includes everything you need to try karting.

Spalding, Lee-Anne T. *Go-Kart Racing.* **Rourke
Publishing, 2008.**

Learn all about the thrill of go-kart racing in this book, written for kids
ages seven and up. Colorful photographs bring this book to life.

More to Explore

All-American Soap Box Derby
http://www.aasbd.org

Learn about the All-American Soap Box Derby, which happens once a year in Ohio, USA. Young racers from all over the United States compete to see who the best racer is.

Kart Building
http://www.kartbuilding.net

This website is a great resource for people who want to build go-karts. There are illustrated and photographic plans for go-karts, including wooden karts and off-road karts.

Do It Yourself
http://www.doityourself.com/stry/how-to-make-a-go-kart

This website contains simple information on how to build a wooden go-kart. Remember, if you want to build a go-kart yourself, you need to have your parents or another adult help you!

Teacher Tube
http://teachertube.com

Teachertube.com is a safe website for your teachers to look up videos to use in your classrooms. You'll find safe and amazing videos on go-karts here.

About the Author

Christine Dugan earned her B.A. from the University of California, San Diego. She taught elementary school for several years before deciding to take on a different challenge in the field of education. She has worked as a product developer, writer, editor, and sales assistant for various educational publishing companies. In recent years, Christine earned her master's degree in education and is currently working as a freelance author and editor. She lives with her husband and two daughters in the Pacific Northwest, where she loves to hit the open road—safely, of course!